Ex

Ribble Valley

Between Ribblehead and Clitheroe

by W. R. Mitchell

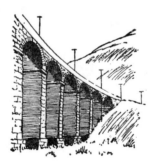

DALESMAN BOOKS
1979

90p.

THE DALESMAN PUBLISHING COMPANY LTD.,
CLAPHAM (via Lancaster), NORTH YORKSHIRE.

First published 1979

© W. R. Mitchell 1979

Cover picture by Fergus Moore

ISBN: 0 85206 561 2

Printed in Great Britain by
GEORGE TODD & SON
Marlborough Street, Whitehaven

Head of
the Dales

WE HAVE LOST the old fear of wild and lonely places. Until well into last century, writers about the upper reaches of the Ribble used words such as "dreadful" and "horrible" to describe the most majestic of the natural features they saw. The historian of Craven, Thomas Dunham Whitaker, had little feeling for natural beauty, and he wrote: "The beauties of Ribblesdale may be said to expire at Horton; for in tracing the course of the Ribble upwards, the woods gradually dwindle, the verdure of the fields diminishes, and the stream becomes a mountain torrent, hurrying along a shallow and desolate valley, which conducts the persevering inquirer to a spring in the ridge of Cam . . ." The admiration of wild country has now become a cult, and for many Horton-in-Ribblesdale is the gateway to their favourite outdoor pleasures.

The river Ribble begins in a wide, north-south valley, buttressed by the fells named Ingleborough (2,373 feet) and Penyghent (2,273 feet). The valley becomes constricted where the Silurian slates obtrude near Stainforth, and the river breaks out from the company of high hills at Settle to course through gentle, park-like country. Water which fell as rain on the high Pennines enters the sea in a six miles wide estuary near Preston.

The upper Ribble lies within the Yorkshire Dales National Park, which was designated in 1954 under the authority of the National Parks and Access to the Countryside Act of 1949. The Pennine Way, Britain's second longest continuous footpath, descends from Penyghent to Horton and then fol-

lows the valley east of the river to cross Cam Fell into
Wensleydale. One does not find a sylvan beauty. The com-
ments of historian Whitaker about the native bleakness
hold good. The head of Ribblesdale can be such a wild area
it is as though the Pleistocene chill is still upon it. Geology
gives a stepped appearance to the valley sides, and there
are plentiful mounds of boulder clay, deposited by ancient
glaciers, these mounds being known as drumlins. Where the
limestone has been bared, forming scars and "pavements,"
it seems that the very bones of the landscape are visible.
The district is pockmarked by "sink holes," where small
potholes have their mouths half-filled with clayey soil, and
streams have a fascinating habit of spending part of their
journey underground, in a network of caves.

High rainfall and poor drainage have led to cold, im-
poverished soils, to peaty moors and tracts of sphagnum
moss. Knoutberry Bank, a feature of Blea Moor, was named
after the cloudberry, an arctic-alpine plant species. Deer
Bank on Cam Fell relates to the time when the undulating
moors were tenanted by herds of red deer. The first men,
entering the district in the wake of the receding ice, doubtless found reindeer summering on the hills.

Many visitors remember Ribblehead as a battleground
of the elements. When the days are hot and sunlit—and
such days do occur—the day-trippers relax on the common
land around the head of the dale, where a T-junction is
formed by the meeting of the Ribblesdale road and the old
turnpike from Lancaster to Richmond. At other times, the
winds are in eager conflict, hurling rain or snow. A wes-
terly gale, roaring up Chapel-le-Dale, has been known to
stop a train as it approached Ribblehead viaduct. Some of
the old farms have their west walls reinforced by corrugated
iron, coated by tar. The average rainfall is some 70 inches,
but in 1954, at the Ribblehead weather station, the amount
recorded was 109 inches.

The hills act like sponges, releasing the water gradually,
into the becks. Batty Moss, across which extends the 24-arch
railway viaduct, must be firmer than it was, for a railway
workman who was here with the first party of surveyors in
the winter of 1869/70 mentioned to a visitor that the accommodation was a four-wheeled caravan. This man stood
beside it with a bull's-eye lantern as a guide to men return-

4

ing wearily across the bogland. Said the old railway worker: "Two chain o' knee-deep water, four times a day, were faced by the fellows atween their meat and their work." It is hardly as bad as that now.

Two mountain becks, Gayle and Cam, combine about half a mile north-east of Selside to form the Ribble. A trickle of water from a cave at so-called Ribblehead satisfies most visitors who like to visit the beginnings of great rivers. Gayle —sometimes rendered Gale—Beck is prominently in view if you approach Ribblehead from Hawes. The road crests at Newby Head which, until 1974, was the boundary between the North and West Ridings. Newby Head, at 1,421 feet, is an important sheep farm that was also an inn. The letters received by "mine host" went via Sedbergh, which lies some 13 miles away.

Gayle Beck flows near the road in an immediate area that is empurpled by heather. Do not be surprised if a red grouse flies off at your approach. Three other local nesting birds are the dipper, ring-ouzel (the white-bibbed "mountain blackbird") and the oystercatcher. The Cam ridge, to your right, is crossed by a grassy track, the Devil's Highway, which is joined by a track from Ribblesdale proper and crosses the watershed to Cam Houses, near the source of the Wharfe. The track was doubtless old when the Romans made use of it, and for a long period it saw the passage of packhorse trains. Summer days on the Devil's Highway are enlivened by the whistling of golden plover, and it is then that cotton grass (which is, in fact, a sedge) whitens the plateaux as though with snow.

The first building you see on your descent from Newby Head to Ribblehead is an old shooting "box" by the beck. Also in view is Ingleborough, one of the big Pennine "flat-tops." Gearstones, where stood another inn, was described by Lord Torrington (1792) as "the seat of misery, in a desert." Each autumn, herds of "black cattle" from the Highlands and Islands of Scotland were driven southwards to the English marts, and a fair of sorts was held at Gearstones. Torrington arrived when "the Scotch fair" was being held upon the heath; the ground in front of the inn was "crowded by Scotch cattle and drovers; and the house cramm'd by the buyers and sellers, most of whom were in plaids, fillibegs, etc." Each Wednesday, we are told by other

5

writers, a market for corn and oatmeal took place at Gearstones. As many as 30 wagons arrived from Wensleydale to provision the farms of upper Ribblesdale and the adjacent valleys.

Gearstones inn featured twice in the story of the railway construction. In the initial stages, a young Tasmanian engineer named Charles Stanley Sharland, a member of the staff of John Crossley, the engineer-in-chief, walked from Carlisle to Settle, taking surveys and levels, and at Gearstones he and six men sheltered from a blizzard, which held them captive for three weeks. In due course, they tunnelled through snow so that they could reach the water trough in the yard. Then, in 1873, a navvy called George Young, while under the influence of strong drink, tossed some dynamite on to the fire at Gearstones, causing injury to some customers and considerable damage to the building. The kettle that had stood before the fire was shattered, and pieces of it were produced in evidence when Young was summoned to Ingleton Court. Near Gearstones, the beck goes out of sight of the road, cutting a deep way through limestone in Thorn's Gill, where a packhorse-type bridge springs from cliff to cliff. It is a venerable bridge, dating from the 17th century. It stood on the line of the Craven Way, between Settle and Dent. It was being well-used long before the main road was made.

Cam Fell, source of the other principal feeder of the Ribble, is a featureless, sodden area. Even a shooting box is an object of significance to the map-makers. The beck flows beneath a single-span bridge which, so a notice proclaims, was repaired in 1766 "at the charge of the whole West Riding." This was on the old road to upper Wensleydale. As at Thorns, the beck has cut deeply into limestone. Cam Beck's gill is named Ling, the name for heather. Sheep had difficulty in reaching many parts of that gill, and there is such floral variety and richness the gill is a nature reserve.

I have not yet mentioned Whernside which, at 2,419 feet, is the highest of the Yorkshire fells. Its cap is composed of millstone grit, and the name Whernside is derived from cweorn (quern), being "the hillside where millstones were obtained." Small farms along the base of Whernside are of Norse origin, and one of them, Bruntscar, became celebrated for a tame trout, which spent part of its life in a subterranean stream and periodically displayed itself to public gaze. I also remember Bruntscar for its cave, which at one time was listed as a "show" system. It is too constricted for the comfort of the average visitor. I had penetrated a good distance, along a passage which forced my body to the shape of a question mark, when I noticed that the water was rising and becoming frothy, the consequences of a storm over Whernside. Where the stream leapt into a small chamber, I had to sit down, temporarily blocking the water. I could feel the level rising up my back, and on leaping down I was accompanied by several tons of water. This countryside is honeycombed with about 1,000 natural shafts and caves, the exploration of which should be left to specialists.

From the summit of Whernside, you have a clear view of Ingleborough (2,365 feet) and Penyghent (2,273 feet). If you decide to undertake a walk to include the summit cairns of these Three Peaks, you would cover a distance of 25 miles and climb a total of some 5,000 feet. This walk is undertaken for pleasure by those who attempt to complete the circuit in 12 hours. Runners and cyclists are also attracted, and for them a time well under three hours is the target. The foot race is held in spring. The cyclo-cross takes place in autumn. The record time is much less than three hours. Those who like to leave a record of their achievement in the district might consider enrolling in the Three Peaks Club of Yorkshire, which is organised from Penyghent Cafe at Horton-in-Ribblesdale.

Among those who regularly visit Ribblesdale are sufferers from Settle-Carlislitis; they have an obsession for the Settle-Carlisle railway. This outstanding railway extends over 72 miles through Ribblesdale and over the tops to the Eden Valley. A viaduct, flanked by two substantial embankments, extends across Batty Moss, carrying the line from a high ledge in Ribblesdale to Blea Moor. The viaduct attains a height of around 100 feet, and of the piers every sixth one is of extra breadth and strength "so that if, from any unlooked for contingency, any one arch should ever fall, only five arches could follow."

Shanty towns to accommodate some 2,000 people lay on and around Batty Green from 1870 to 1876. The foundations of the viaduct were laid on solid rock 25 feet down through peat and clay. Construction work extended from north to south, and a tramway was laid for the transportation of blocks of limestone quarried in Littledale, between the valley and Blea Moor. When six arches of the viaduct were turned, the staging was moved so that work could continue on another six, thus reducing the need for a mountain of timber. A small army of masons received help from a mobile crane that operated on a light timber stage; the crane lifted the big stones into position. As you look at the viaduct, picture the hutments littering the moor, and the various service units, including blacksmith's shop, saw mill, carpenter's shed, stables, pay office and stores. A brickworks was built, the bricks being needed for lining the arches of the viaduct and also the tunnel excavated through Blea Moor. The brickworks had 10 ovens and had a capacity to produce 20,000 bricks a day, the raw material being glacial clay taken from the moss.

The route of the tramway is easily followed, though the lines were lifted a century ago. A trackway extends over Blea Moor, passing three ventilation shafts serving the 2,629 yard long tunnel. Shaft No. 3 has a depth of 390 feet. The work of making Blea Moor Tunnel took place round the clock on weekdays, the terms of the contract forbidding Sunday working except at the special request of the chief engineer. Miners worked in twosomes, one of them holding the jumper (a sharp-ended metal bar used to drill holes for explosives) and the other striking the jumper with a hammer. The man holding the jumper turned it slightly following each blow with the hammer. The workforce had candles for illumination, and in Blea Moor the bill for candles alone was £50 a month. Dynamite was in use, and several miners died from injuries received when, cleaning out old holes with drills, they encountered pieces of unspent dynamite.

When the line was opened, the unsung heroes of the Settle-Carlisle were those who maintained it, including the tunnel gang, members of which lived nearby, some occupying cottages built near the southern entrance to Blea Moor. One of them, a Methodist local preacher, recalls taking a service at Dent. He left home with his bicycle, carried the machine through the tunnel, gained the road at Dent Head and pedalled down to the chapel at Dent Town. Letters for Blea Moor cottages were brought by the postman from Chapel-le-Dale, and groceries from Settle were delivered, once a month, to Ribblehead, from where they were transported by stopping freight train to the remote homesteads. Ribblehead station is used only when the *Dales-rail* passenger service is operating. This service is run by the Dales National Park in conjunction with British Rail. The use of Ribblehead is limited by the fact that the "down" platform was removed to allow rail access to the nearby limeworks.

In its heyday, Ribblehead station received coal and cattle (there was a cattle dock) and despatched to the outer world quarry-stone, wool and farm stock. The whole range of station buildings shone like an advertisement for cleansing fluid. In the office, from 1938 until recent times, the station-master composed coded messages regarding the weather—messages that were transmitted to the Air Ministry. Ribblehead, in highland England, was a valuable link in the chain of weather stations. The stationmaster sometimes released a balloon to assess the height of the cloud base. For years, a harmonium stood in the waiting room and was used for services organised by the local Anglican parson. The station-master's house was reinforced, tiles being laid over walls of dressed stone, to deflect the wild weather. When the annual autumn sales took place, sheep were penned in the approach road to the station.

The head of Ribblesdale is poor farming country; there is much unproductive limestone pavement, and the limestone soils are thin. Glacial clay, overtopped with peat, is spread over large areas. The Norse settlers who arrived 1,000 or so years ago were not in competition in their simple pastoral farming with any other established group of settlers, and Norse names are very common for farmsteads and natural features. Gifts of large tracts of land were made to a number of monasteries, and several farms of today were once monastic granges. Excessive grazing by sheep is largely responsible for the poor condition of the grazings that are seen today. Sheep prevent the natural regeneration of timber, though an exception to the process of denudation is provided by 16-acre Colt Park, on the skirts of the Ingleborough group of fells. Here an ashwood survives over a deeply dissected limestone pavement, and a rich ground flora is seen. The area is now a nature reserve, administered by the Nature Conservancy Council, at Grange-over-Sands. At Colt Park, as in Ling Gill, the sheep found grazing difficult. Over-stocking with sheep has led to the disappearance, from large areas, of the once-plentiful heather. Generations of gamekeepers, by the systematic burning of heather, maintained a fresh young growth for the benefit of red grouse, whose numbers rose beyond the limit tolerated by nature herself. At one time, the Pilkington family, from Lancashire, had the shooting on Blea Moor.

Buildings are comparatively few in number at the top of Ribblesdale. A row of cottages built by the Midland Railway for its servants, and named Salt Lake after an old shanty town, is most conspicuous. The houses are now privately owned. Anyone who stays on the main Ribblesdale road will not see Lodge Hall, or Ingman Lodge, for it is at a lower elevation, being approached by a track that leaves the dale road on the side opposite Salt Lake. Lodge Hall had a monastic origin, being one of many local possessions of Furness Abbey (the ruins of which can be seen near the modern Barrow-in-Furness). After the Dissolution, the Hall was acquired by the Weatherheads, and in 1687 Christopher Weatherhead had his initials incised on a stone above the main door. Carved stone halberds flank the doorway.

Selside is yet another former Norse settlement, the name being said to mean "the croft by the willows." Scribes who compiled the Domesday record counted Selside as the furthest place in Ribblesdale; no reference was made to settlements further north in the dale. Selside came into the possession of Furness Abbey. It lost its sense of remoteness when the Midland Railway brought its line along the edge of the village. An embankment blocks out half the sky. The signal box was removed for preservation elsewhere; that box was manned exclusively by women throughout the 1939-45 war. A nameboard from an old signal box endures as a decoration on the front of a barn—a building which, used for social occasions, was called the Town Hall!

Selside achieved some renown as the nearest settlement to one of the big open shafts of Craven, Alum Pot, on the eastern flank of Simon's Fell, some 1,125 feet above sea level. Terrified 18th century visitors included the Rev. John Hutton, of Kendal, who wrote that "a subterranean rivulet descends into this terrible hiatus, which caused such a dreadful gloom from the spray it raised up as to make us shrink back with horror when we could get a peep into the vast abyss." Alum Pot is like a yawn on the hillside, its top plentifully wooded. Those who peer down into the hole, trying to distinguish rock features in the spray from a water-fall—for a stream flows into the pothole—make out the form of a natural rock bridge. Keep well back from the edge; be content to look from behind a boundary wall.

The first recorded descent, in 1847, saw John Birkbeck, William Metcalfe and 10 others approach Alum through a cave passage called Long Churn. They were equipped with ropes, planks, a turntree and a fire escape belt. Descents from the surface were made later in the century, when the gallant explorers used a windlass, supported by two baulks of timber, a bucket covered with a shield, and ropes to prevent that bucket swinging in mid-air. Among the party of 13 to descend the pothole were three ladies. Latter-day explorers have abseiled down the shaft.

It is an easy walk from Selside to Alum Pot. A small charge is made at the farm for access to the field in which the pothole is indicated by a clump of trees. Most explorers of Alum Pot who stand by the Bridge before making a ladder climb to the lower regions are impressed by the effect of light and vapour in this vast hole. George T. Lowe, describing a descent undertaken by members of the York-shire Ramblers' Club in 1902, wrote thus: "The length of the surface opening is directly north and south, and the sun's rays, now gathering strength, shone on the north end of the huge cavity through a cloud of spray produced by the falling waters of Alum Pot beck, which empties itself into the fissure at the south-west corner. The upper slopes were fringed with trees, whose waving branches sparkling with drops of spray and iridescent colours added to the charm of the weird scene. The vast walls of the pit illumined by the sun were transfigured . . ." Prose of the quality found in the old Ramblers' journals is unknown in these modern days, when reports are little more than lists of statistics.

Alum Pot ends with a dark pool. Read what George Lowe had to write about his feelings on seeing it: "The lip of the final chamber overlooked a black sheet of water, its surface broken by stones, and luckily for us of no great depth. The traverse down to the west side along a black wall brought us to the rough stone-covered floor of a hall about 80 feet high, resonant with the roar of falling water. On our right looking north was a large waterfall some 60 feet high. It fell clear for about 40 feet and then, striking a ledge, broke into spray and completed the leap. The hall measured 60 feet long and 30 feet broad. The west side overhangs considerably. At the northern end, in a quiet pool close to the rock face, the water flows away into the unknown."

In fact, the committee of the Yorkshire Geological and Polytechnic Society in 1901 poured a powder called fluoresein into the water to produce a vivid green stain. Eleven days later the dye was evident in the water at Footnaws Hole, a mile away. On the following day, the dye reached Tarn Dub, which lies a further half mile away. The most surprising fact is that to reach Tarn Dub, the water from Alum Pot flows *under* the river Ribble. In due course, overflowing from Tarn Dub, it enters the river from the direction opposite that where its journey begins.

From Horton to Settle

THE MAIN NORTH RIBBLESDALE VIEWS are crowned by Penyghent. The name of this peak is said to mean "hill of the winds." We do know that the name is Welsh, in a district where Norse terms are the language of topography. "Pen" is Welsh for hill, and this hill is the lowest of the Three Peaks, cresting at 2,273 feet. When viewed from Ribblesdale, it looks like a lion crouching above the dale. Archdeacon Paley, of Giggleswick, thought it resembled a large convex-topped pie. Part of the ridge is called Plover Hill, the name being surely an allusion to the dotterel, now a rare bird in Britain, which must have nested there.

The easiest approach to the summit of Penyghent is from Horton, following the Pennine Way. The lane leads to a shooting hut, near which is Hull Pot, an amphitheatre nearly 300 feet long, 60 feet wide and 60 feet deep. In wet weather a torrent of water pours into the hole, and it is recorded that in particularly wet spells, the stream has filled it to the brim. Normally, the stream goes to ground some way upstream from Hull Pot. Traces of lead, zinc and barytes have been found in the area. Lead for the roof of Horton church is supposed to have been obtained from ore mined at Hull Pot. Hunt Pot, a deep rift, lies not far away. The walker breaks into open ground and climbs to the top of Penyghent on a broad path. In spring, cushions of purple saxifrage adorn the crumbling rocks of the Yoredale Series, and there may be a raven in the air in winter, for the young of birds nesting on the northern Pennines tend to drift southwards when they have attained independence.

The views from the summit, seen by those who walk around (for not all the features can be picked out from one vantage point) include Whernside and Gragareth; the Ingleborough range, Lunesdale and Morecambe Bay and, to the south, the big hump of Pendle Hill. Edmund Bogg, the Victorian writer, would not have needed much persuasion that Penyghent means "hill of the winds." He wrote: "Ugh! how the wind whistles, the mountain grass shivers, the heather and nature assume a sombre hue. Ingleborough appears grim and cold in shadowy outline, as the sun departs, fringing with delectable glimmer the machiolated outlines of cloud-forms, while above are long streaks of pale chrome across a cold, pearly sky. Other snowy cloud-forms are rising, whose very appearance make us shiver with cold."

When Bogg trudged into Horton, he stayed at the *Golden Lion* (no longer an inn, being used today as an outdoor pursuit centre) and later he wrote entertainingly of the motley gathering in the bar—"quarrymen from the limestone quarries, and the dalesmen of the district, thirsty souls, we should imagine, by the amount of beer we saw consumed. Three farmers, who had been to Clapham Fair on that day, were benighted here on our visit; their homes lay some eight or ten miles over the moors, and it would have been sheer foolhardiness to have attempted the journey in the dense darkness of that night. One, an elderly man, who had spent upwards of half-a-century in crossing and re-crossing the moors, attempted the journey; he missed his way, and his horse floundered in a bog, and he was glad to grope his way back to the inn . . ." Ponder on the note of Gothic horror struck by Bogg and others who wrote in the last decade of the 19th century. Nowadays you may find far from terrified visitors on Penyghent on any day of the year.

Bogg's quarrymen, who worked on a small scale, would have been startled if they could have returned to see the Beecroft Quarry of today. Here, men are demonstrating that not only faith moves mountains! In the 18th century, considerable quantities of lime were burned in Ribblesdale. The lime was spread over rough ground to improve it so that it could be stocked by cattle and sheep. Scores of kilns at which lime was burned can be seen in Craven; the stone was quarried in a handy place, and the fuel included coal hewn from the thin, poor seams of the Yoredale rocks. A revolution in quarrying began in Ribblesdale when the Settle-Carlisle railway made it possible for coal to be imported fairly cheaply. The same railway offered the possibility of cheap transportation of lime from the dale to the markets, including the steel works of Sheffield.

Beecroft is the largest quarry in North Ribblesdale. The man who developed that quarry was an Irishman, John Delaney. He and his family left Ireland at the time of the potato famine. John Delaney, settling in Ribblesdale, found employment in the Langcliffe mill of the Christies. He developed some lucrative sidelines, including the carting of coal, and when an ultimatum was issued — he must either restrict himself to work at the mill or leave — Delaney started work on his own account. He read geology at Manchester University and, sustained by capital provided by a Quaker banker in Sheffield, he went into quarrying with such flair that within a short time he had made a fortune. He did not do this by exploiting the men, many of whom were brought in from other areas, including Norfolk. Delaney used to say: "I'd like them to make plenty of money — because then they're making a lot of money for me!" He built a fine house at Settle, and — not caring for Settle tap water — he arranged for water to be drawn from a spring in Beecroft quarry and transported in kits to Settle. The quarry at Beecroft is now owned by I.C.I. Horton-in-Ribblesdale is the "farmstead on dirty land." This is no reflection of the quality of local farming. Indeed, the land between Horton and Stainforth looks dirty when compared with the stretches to the north or south. Here we pass through a countryside where the visible rock is Silurian slate, slabs of which can be seen on the path to the local church. The river bed is of slate — and slate obtrudes on Moughton Fell, at 1,160 feet. Impressive outcrops of Silurian rock are observed near Studfold. The village of Horton extends for over a mile beside the dale road, from which a long cul de sac extends to the east of the river, passing through Newhouses to High Birkwith, with a track leading on to the head of Ling Gill. A forest road, bearing right, extends with others through a vast sitka spruce forest. There is now a crescent of dark green conifers to the north of Penyghent.

You look fairly hard for evidence of old buildings at Horton, though the church is conspicuously ancient and is often photographed from such an angle that Penyghent is seen looming beyond it. At Horton, in monastic times, Jervaulx raised horses (lower down the dale is Studfold, with its clear association with horses), and the church has survived the long years without being ruined. A lych gate gives access to the yard (in which there was once a schoolhouse), and there is Norman work in the structure. Grey pillars, no two of which are similar, support the heavy roof. A piece of stained glass in the west window shows the mitred head of Thomas á Becket. How did it come to find an isolated position in a big window which is predominantly of plain glass? It has been suggested that this and several other pieces of glass were brought to Horton from Jervaulx at the time of the Dissolution, yet the martyr was also known as Sir Thomas of Kent, and descendants of this family are believed to have owned Horton manor in the period after the Dissolution. Could the piece of stained glass be a relatively small survivor from a window raised by the family to the memory of the immortal Becket?

Helwith Bridge spans both rail and river. Some of the local views are not pretty, for quarrying is an untidy operation. At Foredale, limestone taken from the head of Moughton Fell was conveyed in strings of trucks on an incline railway working on a gravity system. You may see the route of this incline, but metals were removed years ago. A row of quarrymen's cottages occupies an unbelievably high situation. The Methodists once held regular services up there. At Coombs quarry the horizontal strata of the limestone is seen to be reclining on the upthrust mudstone of Silurian date. This is the untidy side of Moughton. Approach the fell from Crummockdale, and you pass through an undisturbed limestone countryside in which a mini-forest of juniper brings tonal relief. A raven glides along the scars. From the head of Moughton, you can look across Crummockdale to a majestic Ingleborough.

The Silurian flags of Helwith were once in keen demand. Some were slotted together to hold "soft" water, that water falling on the roofs as rain. Other flags were laid as paths and some immense pieces were placed as divisions between rooms in very old houses. Helwith flags also appeared as tombstones. In quarrying the flags, it was not possible to obtain a square edge with hammer and chisel; the flags, up to 15 feet square, were sawn in a mill.

As first planned, the Settle-Carlisle railway was to have had a station at Helwith, but no station was built. The signal box was removed in 1976. Signalmen had moments of drama, such as when a man was reported to have fallen from an express between Stainforth and Helwith Bridge (he was found in a local inn!) and the day during the 1939-45 war when an ammunition train broke into two at Blea Moor and 30 vans hurtled down the tracks (they eventually stopped of their own accord at Long Preston, some 16 miles from Blea Moor). When a signalman came to relieve a particularly nervous man, he found that the door of the box was securely locked. The occupant had heard the rattling of chains. An inquiry was made. A farmer's dog had escaped from its master and leapt a wall near the signal box; the chain attached to its collar was trapped between capstones, and the rattling occurred as the animal attempted to free itself. Unfortunately, the signalman had not been able to see the dog!

The bogland at Helwith Bridge, on which local quarry enterprises have impinged over the years, has a summertime population of nesting birds, including curlews. The plant life is typical of many another tract of Pennine bogland and includes some of the insectivorous species like sundew. There is evidence that once the river Ribble swung in its course at Helwith Bridge and flowed westwards, being a

Above: Ribblehead viaduct, taking the Settle-Carlisle railway over Batty Moss. Every sixth pier is considerably stronger than the others.

Below: Ingleborough (2,365 ft), viewed from Chapel-le-Dale.

Above: St. Leonard's, Chapel-le-Dale, in the yard of which many railway navvies were buried.

Below: Weathercote House, Chapel-le-Dale, the home of William Metcalfe, a pioneer potholer.

Photo: Cyril Harrington

The Packhorse Bridge in Thorns Gill, near Ribblehead.

Above: Lodge Hall, or Ingman Lodge, near Ribblehead.

Below: Selside, one of the villages which had a Norse foundation.

Above: Penyghent from the air. The hill has a Welsh name in a district where most names are of Norse origin. (Photo: C. H. Wood.)

Below: Penyghent looms beyond the old church of Horton-in-Ribblesdale.

Above: Horton-in-Ribblesdale, looking westwards to Ingleborough. In this part of Ribblesdale, the traveller sees outcrops of slate.

Below: Helwith Bridge and the Ribble. Helwith "flags" were used as containers for rainwater, paths and even tombstones.

Above: Stainforth Bridge, built by Samuel Watson in the 1670s, and now owned by the National Trust.

Below: Stainforth Force, where the Ribble falls into a deep pool.

Above: Stepping stones at Stainforth. The name of this village means "stony ford."

Below: Langcliffe — "the long cliff" — showing fountain and section of the village green. The large building is a Methodist chapel.

tributary of the Lune. In due course, the river broke through Sherwood Brow and took its present course. Swarth Moor was once visited by men from Austwick who carried an important knife, known as a whittle. This was the only knife to be found in the village. The knife was lost on Swarth Moor. The man to whom it was entrusted placed the knife in the ground and, so that he could remember just where it was, he did so at the edge of a cloud shadow!

A metalled road leads west to Austwick. From it you see the few houses of Wharfe set against the steep slopes of Moughton. Eastwards from Helwith Bridge, the old routes are still grassed over. Long Lane runs as straight as a bow-shot towards the nose of Penyghent and then turns towards Dale Head. This white-walled building stands on the line of the Pennine Way and is not far from the base of Ulfgill cross, a monastic boundary marker, at which some of the rebels of the Pilrimage of Grace gathered. Moor Head Lane extends from Helwith to a point near Sannet Hall, giving access to the high grazings and scattered farmsteads of Malham Moor.

You have a choice of routes southwards from Helwith Bridge to Stainforth. There is, indeed, a choice of Stainforths. If you stay west of the river, you will be rewarded, on looking back, with a broad view of Ribblesdale, a view dominated by Penyghent. This road descends between walls to Little Stainforth. The major route, east of the Ribble, rises high on Sherwood Brow, and then descends to Stainforth. Down below, river and railway run close together. The railway engineers contrived to divert the water. Their line ran on the old river bed!

Between the two Stainforths, the river is spanned by a single-arch packhorse bridge. Stainforth Bridge, which since 1931 has been owned by The National Trust, was built in the 1670s by Samuel Watson, a much-persecuted Quaker who lived at Knight Stainforth Hall. His family had bought Knight Stainforth in 1547, and his gift of a bridge was appreciated, for Stainforth owes its name to the former river crossing, the "stony ford." Up to the year it was handed over to the Trust, the owner of the Hall had been responsible for the bridge's repair. At Stainforth Force, below the bridge, the Ribble tumbles into a deep hole which has a sense of mystery imparted by the tumbling water and the shadows provided by riverside trees. This district had two ghosts—a man and a dog—which nightly wandered from Knight Stainforth to Dog Hill.

A modern map shows Stainforth and Little Stainforth, separated by the Ribble. The old divisions were Friar Stainford and Knight Stainford. The friars were associated with Sawley Abbey, which was established much lower down the dale. The knights were members of the Tempest family, from whom the manor passed to the D'Arcys. They sold it to the Watson family in 1547. I have already mentioned the benevolence of Samuel Watson in providing a bridge; he also re-built the old hall, and if you look at it today you will immediately notice that several windows have been blocked up, a consequence of the unhygenic "window tax."

Cowside Beck, flowing off Malham Moor, tumbles in spectacular fashion in a narrow little ravine to the east of Stainforth. Catrigg Force rivalled in appeal the fall below Stainforth Bridge. Visitors to Catrigg were assisted in their descent to the base of the fall by the provision of over 60 steps and a handrail. Among the Victorian visitors was the composer Edward Elgar. He had formed a deep friendship with a Settle doctor, C. W. Buck, and regularly visited Ribblesdale. An old name for the waterfall was Catterick. Elgar wrote to Buck in January 1887, acknowledging the gift of a photograph. He stated: "Catterick Force is duly installed in a place of honour next to Scaleber (received last year) and the violence done to Settle geology is more than recompensed by the pretty contrast presented."

One of the most adventurous Dales roads begins at Stainforth under the prosaic title of "Goat Lane." The goats must have been of the mountain variety! This route, which has been improved in recent years, passes near the grey scars of Silverdale to Dale Head and the area "back o' Penyghent." On the east of the road is Fountains Fell, named after a former association with the abbey of that name. High on Fountains are a tarn and a group of shafts. Coal was mined in the Yoredale rocks, and the old Coal Road zigzags down the fellside. To be on Fountains Fell as evening comes on a day in May is an unforgettable experience—granted that the weather is sunny. The westering sun has put Penyghent into deep shadow, yet strong rays pick out the heathery cap of Fountains and enhance the rich hue of the sedges growing on the slopes. Through the still, crisp air comes the delicate trilling of a dunlin, a bird which nests on Fountains Fell. The dunlin is known as "plover's page" because of its inclination to nest in the same areas as the golden plover. The dunlin's special requirement is for soggy moorland, especially high ground where there are pools of water, a qualification that is met by Fountains Fell. The bird is confiding, and you may walk fairly close to it with care. Finding a dunlin nest is one of the most difficult tasks facing an ornithologist.

Gingling Hole, between Fountains Fell and Silverdale, has a place in the history of human enterprise in North Craven. It was here, in the autumn of 1934, that one or two cheerful volunteers brought to the surface a man who had fractured a leg during a potholing expedition. In February of the following year, the Central Potholing Rescue Corps was formed. It became the Cave Rescue Organisation. For some 20 years, rescues were few and far between, but with the increase in the number of visitors, both potholers and fell-walkers, there is now a call-out about once a week! The C.R.O. is the fellside equivalent of the lifeboat service at sea.

Winskill Scar, a feature dominating the valley between Stainforth and Langcliffe, was given its present shape by man — and the weather. What you see is a former quarry, the excavated area of which is now being filled with rubbish by the local authority. Winskill was a farmhouse, the home of Tom Twisleton, who acquired renown as a poet. One of his works, published in 1867, was entitled "Splinters Struck Off Winskill Rock." Born at Dent, Tom arrived above Ribblesdale with his father and mother when he was young, and farming was his main job. He developed into a huge fellow, over six feet in height, bulky in proportion, but of considerable stamina. His poetic works touch on a variety of subjects — letters to his brother and various friends, the death of a workman during the construction of the Settle-Carlisle line, an incident when both barrels of his gun failed to go off, or as an accompanying note sent with an insurance policy to a lady who was afraid of fire! Tom was a staunch teetotaller, and over half his poems touched upon the evils of strong drink. For a short time after his removal from Winskill, he lived at Burnsall, from where he penned two or three poems, and later he removed to Burley, where he died in 1917. Tom Twisleton wrote:

Pray, pardon me, if now I raise
A stave or two to sound the praise
Of Craven's hills and caves;
Of fertile daals an' flowin' brooks,
Of water-faus an' shady nooks,
Whar t'fir and' t'hazel waves.

Whar cliffs uprear their shaggy waus,
And down below a streamlet flows,
Wi' rough and blusterin' din;
While masses of projectin' rock
Owerhing as if the slightest shock
Wad send 'em thunderin' in.

Craven Quarry was being developed when the Settle-Carlisle railway came to Ribblesdale. Lime was being taken from it by rail before the entire route to Carlisle was open for traffic. It is related by a former locomotive driver that one day, during the 1939-45 war, his fireman was a young chap who had been trained in the area around York. The driver told him he had not sufficient fire. In due course — as they passed Stainforth — he pointed to the quarry chimney, which has now been demolished. "In 20 miles we'll have reached the height o' that chimney," he declared. The fireman, taking the hint, began to shovel coal furiously!

What remains is a remarkable piece of industrial archaeology. The old quarry-owner ordered a Hoffman's kiln, of German design. This kiln, devised for continuous burning, was 150 feet long, 48 feet wide, with 16 chambers, each capable of holding 190 tons of stone. Each chamber had 36 feeding holes, amounting to 576 for the whole kiln. Alas, it was "labour intensive" and more economical kilns were later introduced to the quarries of the dale. The shell of the kiln remains. It is worthy of preservation.

Langcliffe, the village of the "long cliff," snuggles deep in the shelter of the scars, away from the bite of easterly gales. Langcliffe is the village with a green, and it sends a road daringly up the hillside to Malham Moor. Those who have the energy to walk up that road, to Clay Pits Plantation, can then follow a lane leading to the scars and Victoria Cave, one of the big "bone caves" of England. From Victoria Cave, and others nearby, came much evidence of life in the district in remote times. The cave was re-discovered after many centuries of obscurity by Michael Horner, who lived at Langcliffe. In May 1838, he and two other young men were on the scars when they met John Jennings, of Settle, who was accompanied by two terriers. Jennings suggested that they might go to some holes where foxes were known to lie up.

One of the terriers was put into the lower hole, and in due course it appeared at the mouth of another hole. The young men and terriers were back at the Fox Holes a week later; they dragged away a large stone, forming an opening that was large enough to admit Michael Horner. He told his employer, Joseph Jackson, about his discovery, and the two men explored the cave by night. They entered a large chamber that was bedecked by stalactites. In the following weeks, as the cave became well-known, the limestone formations were taken away by local people.

Joseph Jackson went on to discover remnants of life in the distant past. He concluded that the cave had been unknown to humankind for well over 1,000 years. Later, with Professor W. Boyd Dawkins and R. H. Tiddeman, of the Geological Survey, there was an organised but spasmodic excavation of Victoria Cave — as it became known, having been found in Coronation year. Objects taken from the cave dated back to an inter-glacial period, when the district's fauna included straight-tusked elephant, slender-nosed rhinoceros, wooly hippopotamus and the ox *Bos primigenius*. The remains of hyena implied that Victoria Cave was then a hyena den. The excavators found clay deposited at the end of the Ice Age, above which was the fauna of a tundral period, when the landscape was frequented by reindeer, arctic fox, badger and wild horse. The cave remains told of early hunters, one of whom left in this sanctuary a reverse barbed harpoon, indicating that fish were being taken from the glacial lakes. The last group of cavefolk, of Romano-British times, probably used the cave as a burial area, judging from the moderately large number of attractive objects found. They included silver and bronze brooches, Roman coins and spearheads. Such caves were unlikely to be used for habitation, except perhaps for brief periods in winter. Several caves on the scars have yielded evidence of early human and animal life, and from Kinsey Cave, on Giggleswick Scars, was removed the skull of the great cave bear.

Langcliffe has a magnificent hall, on the doorway of which is a stone dated 1602, which clearly relates to an earlier structure. For generations, the Dawson family resided at Langcliffe Hall, and here — for two long spells — lived Geoffrey Dawson, who edited *The Times*. The story is told that at one time he and an aunt occupied the building. When his newspaper in London wished to contact him, they had to telephone Settle, from whence a runner was despatched to Langcliffe. Auntie would not allow a telephone to be installed in her home!

George H. Brown related that from 1854 until 1859 was a time of tribulation at Langcliffe. "The Mills were stopped; families left, and many houses were empty; streets became grass-grown, and it seemed likely that Langcliffe must be called 'the deserted village.' But the purchase of the Mills by Mr Lorenzo Christie gave life again to the place. The village was largely re-peopled by families from Norfolk and Cornwall, and as these are two strongly Methodistic counties, the Wesleyans have since then had at Langcliffe a large and active society." Langcliffe church dates from the period immediately before the period of slump. Mr. Hector Christie, who succeeded at Langcliffe mills, was a devout Anglican, and in 1868 he gave to the church a fine stained-glass window.

Walk down a road from Langcliffe towards the river and you will find yourself on an island, a tract of land occupied by Locks Cottages. On one side is the Ribble, and on the other the mill dam. There are modest flows of water from the river and back into it, completing the island flavour. The dam is the haunt of semi-domesticated ducks, and at the inflow is a hut used by the Water Authority's fishery department, who here intercept migratory salmon at a fish pass. The run of salmon and sea trout up the Ribble once stopped at the big dam at Settle. The salmon would have been capable of clearing this obstruction if they had some depth of water from which to spring, but below Settle dam lay thick slabs of limestone. The dam was provided with a fish-pass, and shortly afterwards similar attention was given to Langcliffe dam. Consequently, the fish now spawn far up the dale.

A footbridge at the Locks enables pedestrians to cross to the Stackhouse side of the river. The present bridge replaced one which was washed away in a flood during 1953. A walk from Settle to the bridge, and back into Settle on the other side of the river, has a continuous appeal, even to local people. Stackhouse is a secluded village. Its large houses are set in a wooded area. A Victorian visitor wrote: "A few gentry have settled beneath its wooded scars, practical farming combined with peaceful retirement being their portion for ever." Stackhouse is by no means a new settlement. One house is dated 1695, and the hamlet was the home of two notable families, the Carrs and Brayshaws. The Carrs were principal tenants of Furness Abbey, John Carr being virtually the founder of Giggleswick School. In the 1860s William Carr was reported to have bred a fine herd of cattle and to have written a study of the Shorthorn breed.

A footpath sign on the Settle side of Stackhouse points to the high scars. Follow the path, and you will find yourself on Giggleswick Scars, in an austere limestone world. The extensive views take in the ridges of Bowland and, north-eastwards, you see Penyghent. In another direction, Ingleborough is prominently in view. Giggleswick Scars dominate the A65, more precisely the stretch known as Buckhaw Brow. (Quarrymen are nibbling at the southern end of the limestone range; they used to send stone in buckets, by overhead ropeway, to Giggleswick station.)

The road extends along the line of a geological fault, as you may see if you study the walls. On one side of the road they are grey (limestone) and on the other a variety of darker hues (millstone grit). There is a mottling effect as the two types of stone intermingle about the area of the road. The effect of the fault is dramatic if you remember that limestone is normally far below the millstone grit.

On the Scars is the Schoolboys' Tower, constructed by scholars at Giggleswick School. The lower slopes of this limestone ridge are now well-wooded, and within the woodland is Nevison's Nick, which is associated (in legend only) with a ubiquitous northern highwayman who is said to have leapt across it. At the roadside, deep in the shadow of trees, stands the Ebbing and Flowing Well. There appears to be a double-syphon in the rock, and the water ebbs and flows in a stone trough by the road. There is no guarantee that you will see the well operating. The Rev. Theodore Brocklehurst, vicar of Giggleswick for over three decades, was fond of visiting the well, but he saw it working on only two occasions. Times of moderate rainfall appear to be the best periods for observation. Some years ago, investigation by boys from Giggleswick school revealed that the temperature of the water in the well was virtually unchanging throughout the year, even during a notoriously cold winter. It was never lower than 8.1 deg. C nor higher than 9.0 deg. C.

At Giggleswick Church is stained glass commemorating the patron, Saint Alkelda. The glass is quite modern. The pictures it forms are of the Ebbing and Flowing Well—first the spirit of the well, and then the saint herself baptising converts in its water. (A third picture shows the death of Alkelda, strangled by "heathen women" as she journeyed from Giggleswick to Middleham, in Wensleydale. Middleham is the only other church to be dedicated to her.) An ornate bucket at Giggleswick Church is said to have been used to bring water from the Ebbing and Flowing Well for baptisms. Did Alkelda exist? Or was she just a nature spirit, of great age, who was "converted" to Christianity? "Keld" appears in her name—and keld is an old word for spring.

The Well is less of an attraction to visitors than it was, possibly because of the difficulty in parking a car at a time when the road hums to the continual passing of traffic. Michael Drayton, visiting the district over 300 years ago, had the time and opportunity to stand and stare:

> At Giggleswick where I a fountain can you show,
> That eight times a day is said to ebb and flow.

Richard Braithwaite noted, in the 17th century:

> Neither know the learned that travel,
> What procures it, salt or gravel.

A horseman watered his steed at the Well, just as the trough was on the point of emptying itself. He had not heard of the special properties, and concluded—when the trough was empty—that the horse had drunk 15 gallons of water in a few seconds. In 1840, two Americans hired workmen to dismantle the Well and replace the pieces. The Rev. George H. Brown, of Settle, set himself the task of walking to the Well every day during 1899. Sometimes he arrived as early as 5 a.m. He spent an hour a day studying the Well's conduct and several times, chiefly during June, he saw the "silver chord," a string of bubbles caused by an air current passing through the water.

Settle and Giggleswick

A KNOLL OF LIMESTONE, dominating the town of Settle, has the imposing name of Castleberg. It was once a handy source of limestone, exploited by quarrymen. In due course, there were local objections, and the quarrying stopped. A pen and ink drawing of "The Shepherd's Dyal" showed grey flagstones set on the face of old Castleberg, each stone incised with a Roman numeral. The knoll was then stated to serve as a giant sundial. Bishop Pococke saw four large stones *in situ* and wrote that the sundial benefited "the country for three or four miles southward, as they know what hour of the morn it is when the shadow comes to them, from 9 to 12." Once open for public enjoyment, Castleberg was out of bounds for some years until the parish council acquired the rights to it and cleaned it up. Since then, the slopes have been planted with trees. A zig-zag path leads to the crest of the rock, where stands a flagpost. Settle, Giggleswick, and the countryside for miles around, is spread before the visitor. The high point of a gritstone ridge to the west is Whelpstone Crag (a name suggesting it was once frequented by wolves). Early this century, Harwood Brierley won "the beetling brow of Castleberg," "noticing that the whole of the Frenchy-looking little town is seen below. It is said the very houses can be counted, and at eventide, when Castlebergh is illuminated by the westering sun, its face is veiled by blue smoke curling up from the little town, giving it some of the glamour of an eminence in Rhineland."

To the people of Old Settle, a town clustered around the base of Castleberg, there was once a real fear that the rock itself might fall and crush them. Until remedial work was carried out, there were periodical falls of stone, usually after times of severe frost, and in modern times the minister of Zion Congregational Church went to an insurance agent, seeking to insure the building against damage from falling boulders. He was told, gravely, that if boulders hit the chapel it would be an "act of God"! George Brown, a former minister at Zion, recorded that in 1883 "two large stones lost their hold and came bounding down the hill. The smaller one crashed through the wall behind the chapel, and damaged the choir-window. The other, at least a ton and a half in weight, dropped into the yard behind the National School, where it still lies (1896). This sort of bombardment was alarming enough, and not least to the writer of these pages who had to stand twice every Sunday in the pulpit of the said chapel. If the larger of the two stones had been the one to strike the chapel, and during service-time, the tune would have become a short metre, or the sermon have been brought to a too impressive end."

The Domesday scribes recorded the existence of Settle, and in medieval times a number of abbeys claimed parts of the district. Centuries of ploughing on the slopes led to the appearance of the long strip field systems which are still prominent. Before the turnpike road was opened, the road from Skipton to Long Preston followed a moorland route, which was described thus by John Ogilby, the 17th century map-maker: "Crossing a Stone-Bridg and Brook you enter *Long Preston,* a village of 5 Furlongs extent and some Entertainment; at the end whereof you enter a Moor, and ascend an Hill of 10 Furlongs height, and presently descend again 8 Furlongs at the bottom of which you enter *Settle,*

34

a Town of good Accommodation enjoying a Market on Tuesdays." At Hunter Bark, the moorland road achieved an elevation of 1,025 feet; it was a route not undertaken lightly in the depth of winter. Today, it is regarded as a pleasant walking track. Some Settle folk trudge along it to Long Preston and return to town by bus.

Settle, which suffered a measure of isolation, lying between high hills and the Ribble marshes, began to develop when the turnpike road was completed in 1754; from then until the coming of the railway in 1848 there was considerable building in durable stone. Incidentally, the old road entered Upper Settle and descended Kirkgate to the river, making use of the old bridge. The Ribble was negotiable to foot traffic at Kendalman's Ford, below the King's Mill, traffic proceeding along a narrow lane into Giggleswick. Traditionally, "mine host" of a former inn called *The Travellers' Rest* provided a man to guide wayfarers across Kendalman's Ford at night. It is believed that Belle Hill, the name for the steep descent from the A65 into the village, is derived from a bell that was maintained for the same purpose. The bridge at Settle is old, but packhorses and pedestrians used the ford when the river was low as a short cut, avoiding the hill on the Giggleswick side of the river bridge. Not until 1804 was the turnpike improved by being extended direct from the market place to the river. (The parish church was not built until the 1830s.)

Some 20 years after the coming of the turnpike road, a canal was projected. Those who advanced the idea drew attention to the "great quantities of goods and merchandise" that "now passes by land-carriage at a very great expense from London, Hull, Sheffield, Leeds, Halifax, through Settle to Kendal and the n.w. parts of this kingdom, and of heavy manufactured goods from Kendal to the London market and other places." No canal was built, and Settle continued to exist at a modest size. It was, none the less, an important centre for the tanning industry, hides being dressed in the town, and leather-dealers arriving in number during the 18th century, at the time of the August Fair. Cattle and sheep were displayed for sale in the market place, and when the October Fair was held in 1859 about 20,000 sheep were sold. Pictures recall a time when Settle had a goose fair. The birds, reared on farms in the locality, were driven in on foot, and in some cases their webbed feet were reinforced against the roughness of the road. The geese were driven through pools of tar!

The Birkbecks of Anley were associated with Settle's business life, being major shareholders in the Craven Bank, which they established in conjunction with the Alcocks of Skipton. Castleberg, the limestone knoll, was pictured on some of the banknotes. Of the buildings noted on the tithe map of 1844, the Folly is outstanding, being a large house, with many novel features for its time, built by the wealthy tanner Richard Preston in the prosperous 1670s. The Town Hall, which replaced the Tolbooth in the 1830s, is of a fanciful style which has been described as Jacobean Gothic! Richard Hardacre, a poet of Long Preston, looked at the new structure and wrote some verse, ending:

> It's topping, gallant, noble, fine,
> And has been building two years' time,
> About it now I'll say no more,
> I ne'er saw such a place before.

On its erection, it was stated to include a "market-house, newsroom, public library, savings bank, &c." For many years until 1974, it was used as the headquarters of the Settle Rural District Council, which administered a considerable tract of land — a tract roughly the size of the Isle of Man.

Of the local inns, the *Naked Man* was so named as a skit on the excessive clothing tastes of the time. The *Golden Lion* was moved round the corner from Cheapside into Duke Street (formerly Duck Street) when the turnpike arrived, the proprietor wishing to take advantage of the new surge of traffic. The *Royal Oak* remains, but the *White Horse,* which stood just across the road from it, is now only a memory. So is the *Spreadeagle Hotel,* which stood in Kirkgate. The Shambles survive as a distinctive range of local buildings, though the cottages of two storeys were introduced during a late Victorian restoration; they had been of single storey.

A former inn to be mentioned in connection with the coming of the railway was the *New Inn.* When the Little North-Western company laid tracks from Skipton to Ingleton, they were soon some little distance from the town centre. The railway was opened in 1848, and in 1849 the company purchased the *New Inn* and its associated buildings. These were demolished, creating Station Road. The wide road extended across the valley to what was then Settle station. It was re-named "Giggleswick" when Settle itself appeared on the railway map in the 1870s, with the coming of the Settle-Carlisle line. This railway, its viaducts and embankments, cut Settle into two parts, as you can most clearly see if you view the town from Castleberg. Just beyond the tracks is the green oblong of Settle cricket ground. A hoary story relates that a batsman hit a ball for over 72 miles, the ball being driven through the window of a passing train and being picked up at Carlisle!

Settle is now a bright, well-kept town. Co-operation between the council, traders and civic society led to a central "face-lift." It had previously been unkempt, and an 18th century visitor, Thomas Gray, likened it to "a shabby French town." Settle is most colourful and gay on Tuesdays, when stalls take root in the market place and tradesmen, many of them from Lancashire, add a dash of northern humour to their sales talk. On Tuesdays, the townsfolk, countryfolk and many summer visitors jostle in the market, gossiping as well as shopping.

Settle has scenic variety. It lies between the limestone of North Craven and the gritstone of the Bowland ridges; between a broad and verdant Ribble Valley and the narrowing reaches of the upper dale; between the Long Drag (as the railway is known from Settle Junction to its crest at Ais Gill) and the Short Drag (as one might term the A65, rising grandly along the edge of Giggleswick Scars). Incidentally, the turnpike trustees chose this route in preference to the old way, which crossed High Rigg above Giggleswick. What is now called Buckhaw Brow was once simply "the back lane."

The river Ribble divides the parishes of Settle and Giggleswick, and Giggleswick is far and away the older community. Until the construction of a church at Settle, the parish of Giggleswick embraced the town. Giggleswick has a more sheltered site, being low, on the banks of Tems Beck. In times of heavy rain, when the streams from Giggleswick Scar are in lusty spate, the area round Giggleswick floods, a major stretch of water lying where, until the 1830s, there stood a tarn. From five feet below the bed of the drained tarn, in 1863, workmen removed a dug-out canoe that was some eight feet long and two feet wide. The boat was moved to Leeds Museum, and it perished in an air raid on the city during the 1939-45 war. Five townships met on Giggleswick Moor (1,100 feet), the boundaries radiating from the Resting Stones on Black Hill. Years ago, when moor and moss inhibited much travel, a hard causeway was laid across Cocket Moss, near Wham, and it may still be followed with care by those who are familiar with the route. Others may find themselves waist deep in slime!

Giggleswick is said to have been a Scandinavian settlement (named after the *wick* of one Gikel), and its church dates back to the early 12th century. Though several times extended, and several times restored, it has not lost the atmosphere of antiquity. It would be tedious to catalogue its many fine features, but visitors show much interest in the stained glass, of Victorian date, set in the west window, showing the Ebbing and Flowing Well, St. Alkelda baptising converts here, and the death of Alkelda on her way to Middleham.

The village is dominated by a range of buildings connected with Giggleswick School. Houses at the School bear the names of those who contributed greatly to its development from the 16th century: Carr, Nowell, Shute, Paley, Style, Morrison. James Carr was the first schoolmaster, having leased half an acre of ground near the churchyard for "one gramer schole," which is thought to have been a modest cottage of two storeys. John Nowell, who was a vicar of Giggleswick as well as schoolmaster, secured for the School its Royal Charter, in 1553, and thus there came into being the "Free Grammar School of King Edward VI at Giggleswick." This school was "for the erudition and instruction of children and young men." The School flourished under Shute, and William Paley, who was headmaster from 1744 to 1798, established some valuable University fellowships and scholarships. (Dr. G. A. Butterton, 1846-59, who re-built the old school in 1851, is uncommemorated in the list of houses.)

The Rev. George Style's headship was notable for the construction of the present large buildings, and the most recent house is named Morrison, after Walter Morrison, of Malham Tarn House, a former pupil of the school who became an exceedingly rich man. It was Morrison who eyed a gritstone knoll standing above School and village and offered to the governors a Jubilee memorial chapel that would be something special: a building in the shape of a Latin cross, surmounted by an Oriental dome of cement, terra cotta, wood and sheet copper, the height to be 92 feet, at which elevation there would be a stone lantern and cross of gilded metal. Mr. T. Graham Jackson drew the plans, and the foundation stone was laid in October 1897. Just a year later, the Bishop of Ripon preached the opening sermon. The chapel is prominent and distinctive. It is related that a villager, seeing it during the course of construction, observed: "What do they want buildin' a heeathen temple up yon? Sewerly t'owd church were good anuff for t'skewl lads to say their prayers in!"

The road passing near the chapel is that ancient highway crossing High Rigg. From it can be seen the full range of Giggleswick Scars. The most conspicuous feature is the rapidly-expanding limestone quarry. In June 1927, when the total eclipse of the sun was expected, the Astronomer Royal selected Giggleswick for the Royal Society's observations. The camera he used to record the eclipse was 45 feet long. The sun had a last minute tussle with cloud, but then it shone. At 6h 24m 26sec, on June 29, an estimated 100,000 people had assembled in the district for a sight that would not return to Yorkshire until 1999. Among the guests in the grounds of Giggleswick School were Ramsay Macdonald, Sir James Barrie and Sir John Simon.

Away from the Fells

BELOW SETTLE AND GIGGLESWICK, the Ribble Valley is broad and relatively flat. The hills stand well apart, and the few farmsteads are high up, clear of the periodical flooding of an area which, in immediate post-glacial times, must have held a string of lakes. These degenerated into the marshland which was the bane of early travellers, who were forced to keep to the hill routes.

Becks which have their sources high on the hills tumble down the slopes to join the Ribble. On the east lies the secluded valley of Stockdale, approached from the Settle-Malhamdale road. Stockdale, which was given to Sawley Abbey by Richard de Morville, has a single habitation, a large sheep farm specialising in the Swaledale breed. A track leads up Stockdale and over the tops to Malham. The beck runs along the line of the Mid-Craven Fault, and so the limestone which is so spectacular on Attermire has a sudden visible termination low in the dale. So austere is little Stockdale that carrion crows with few trees available, have been known to nest on walltops. Stockdale Beck becomes Scaleber Beck, and Scaleber Force (which lies only a few paces from the motor road) is the point at which the water takes an impressive leap into a wooded gorge. Elgar was among the Victorian visitors to this waterfall.

Down in the valley, the A65 passes under a bridge of the Settle-Carlisle line, in the area of Old Anley and Cleatop. Old Anley (now a barn) was a fine 17th century house. On the site, at the time of the Norman Conquest, was the home of the old Lord of Settle. Nearby Cleatop was once owned by the Percy family, but Cleatop land was leased towards the end of the Middle Ages to the Proctors and the Tennants; it was sold in 1616 by the fourth Earl of Cumberland to Sir Robert Bindloss, a Kendal merchant. The long railway embankment, at the start of the Settle-Carlisle railway, demonstrates by its steepness the severity of a system on which the ruling gradient for 22 miles is 1 in 100.

Use the road running to the west of the Ribble, from Giggleswick to Rathmell, and the soggy nature of the valley is soon apparent. Drainage is impeded by boulder clay which has a depth of up to 20 feet. The best views are to be obtained from the east, using the higher ground, but on the west the features of the flood plain are at closer range. There are impressive ox-bows. The valley is outstanding for its wild birds. Thousands of birds, of the wader families, gather here after the nesting season, broadcasting frayed

Above: Knight Stainforth Hall, west of the river. Two ghosts, a man and his dog, are said to frequent the area.

Below: Victoria Cave, on the scars high above Langcliffe, yielded evidence of early animal and human life in the district.

Above: Upper Settle, snuggling against limestone hills, as it was before much of the lower ground was developed.

Below: Tems Beck, at Giggleswick, beside which there is a short but picturesque walk.

Above: Attermire Scars, from Stockdale, a lonely valley close to Settle. (Photo: E. Horner.)

Below: St. Alkelda's church, at Giggleswick, once presided over a huge parish.

Above: These buildings at Rathmell were formerly connected with a Nonconformist college.

Below: The Reading Room at Rathmell, a village standing well clear of the Ribble floods.

Above: Long Preston, which extends along either side of the A6. The name of this village is derived from "long priest's town."

Below: Cow Bridge, spanning the Ribble between Long Preston and Wigglesworth.

Above: Wigglesworth, which once had pretensions to being a spa.

Below: Hellifield was a notable railway centre. This old print shows the shed of the Lancashire and Yorkshire Railway.

Above: The church at Bolton-by-Bowland, which is associated with the Pudsay family.

Below: Waddington church, on the northern side of the Ribble.

Above: Browsholme Hall, historic Bowland home of the Parker family.

Below: Memorial to the Craven historian, Dr. T. D. Whitaker, in Whalley church.

feathers during the moult. Autumn skies are a-wirl with curlews, lapwings and golden plover. I remember the *kleep* of oystercatchers with nests on shingle and pastureland, teal springing from a pond to perform acrobatics with all the zest of waders, and the sighting of uncommon migrant waders: greenshank, green sandpiper, little stint and ruff. When the Ribble Valley is flooded in winter, it is not long before Bewick's or whooper swans, in small family parties, plane down to feed and rest.

The farms of this area were built beside springs of water at points central to the land over which they preside. Each has a broad belt of land, from riverside to felltop, and each takes advantage of the different qualities of soil. Most of the flood control work in the valley was enacted between 1799 and the 1850s. In 1799 an Act was obtained to allow parts of Long Preston parish to be enclosed, and this Act had, in addition to the usual provisions, a number of unusual clauses relating to the drainage of the lower riverside meadows and pastures, and the embanking and control of streams and river. In 1856, it was becoming clear that the work was on too small a scale. The banks of the main river needed much attention. Another flurry of activity began. From documents connected with the drainage one discovers the field names, some of which terminate with –holme, signifying that the land was marshy. The Old Norse holmr means "low-lying ground by a stream." Merebeck, a prominent farm high on the eastern side of the valley, took its name from an old demarcation, "meer" signifying a boundary. On the western side of Ribblesdale, a floodbank extends from Hollin Hall Barn to Cow Bridge. The floodbank on the eastern side starts near the bridge that carries the railway across the river. Until myxomatosis swept through the district, rabbits were a considerable pest, for they burrowed into, and sometimes through, the floodbanks.

When the Ribble surges to the top of the banks, it is running five feet above normal. In really wet spells—say, once every 10 years—the river spills over the banks and gives the valley something of its old lakeland status. Until the raising of the level of the road near Rathmell Brow, the road frequently flooded when the river had backed up, impeding drainage from the hills. The Ribble is capable of rapid rise, but the water level soon falls, and there remains a valley enriched by silt brought down from the high hills. Flooding can be bad when south-west winds drive rain on to the peaks at the head of Ribblesdale; if the wind moves to the north-west, conditions clear up almost immediately. The farmers have to be especially sensitive to the weather, and if on a winter evening the rain is being borne on a south-west wind they expect a flood and drive their stock from the lowest ground. Walls can be badly damaged when they are standing deep in water and — as invariably happens in these circumstances — a wind springs up. The damage is caused by wave action.

The Ribble Valley consists of good land. Towards Giggleswick there is a loam over gravel, with four feet of soil in most places, though lower down — towards Long Preston — there is some moss-type land, with an underlay of impervious clay. One farmer, with 74 acres of what seemed to be irretrievable marsh, rodded-out some blocked drains and was subsequently able to re-seed over 30 of these acres. The valley is for mixed farming. Store cattle are fattened on the pastureland. When the meadows have been cleared of hay or grass for silage, the "fog" (second flush of grass) sustains the dairy animals and also fattens the sheep and lambs.

The threat of a reservoir has, for years, hung over the valley between Settle and Hellifield. The water authority has shown an interest in the possibility of making a river-regulating reservoir. The river would be assured of a certain flow, and the water would be taken out lower down, avoiding the necessity for laying large pipes. What has been envisaged for this part of the valley is a lake four miles long, a mile wide, and 25 feet in depth in places. By good fortune, the water engineers located two outcrops of rock in a gorge below Cow Bridge where a small dam could be made. Such a dam would fit like a cork in a bottle. If a reservoir is constructed — and the farmers have objected strongly — it would be necessary to re-route the main road and railway.

Rathmell is like a village on a headland, high above the areas that flood. At Rathmell, in about 1670, Richard Frankland established the first nonconformist college in England. Frankland was born in the village in 1630, and he attended Giggleswick School, obtaining a scholarship to Christ's College, Cambridge, in 1648. Because of his strong views, he was ex-communicated at Giggleswick, and so the college came into being. Persecution was ceaseless, and from time to time he had to change his residence, but he succeeded in educating and training 304 students for the dissenting ministry. Towards the end of his life, tolerance was shown towards him by the Established Church. He received absolution, and when he died in 1698 he was interred in the yard at Giggleswick church. Subsequently, the Rathmell college was moved to Manchester, to London and then to Oxford.

In earlier times, the Hammertons lived in great style at Wigglesworth Hall, which had a deer park. The main approach was a splendid carriage drive, over half a mile long, that began above Cow Bridge. The Hammertons were a power in Craven from the 12th century. They showed the usual benevolence towards the church, and Stephen, son of Hugh of Hammerton, gave 20 cartloads of hay to the monks of Kirkstall. Adam de Hammerton married the granddaughter of Elias de Knoll, who held Hellifield and Wigglesworth, and so the Hammertons acquired land and property in this fertile part of the Ribble Valley. By a series of judicious marriages, they acquired vaster estates until it was their boast that they could ride from Hammerton all the way to York on their own land. Their end came dramatically. Sir Stephen Hammerton joined the commons in the Pilgrimage of Grace, for which he was hanged. On the day of the execution his only son, Henry, died of grief. Today, the remaining old buildings at Wigglesworth are divided into two farmhouses. A soke mill which stood by the beck close at hand was demolished in 1860. The great barn — once one of the wonders of Ribblesdale — was gutted by fire in recent times. Thoresby, in 1694, had described the barn he saw at Wigglesworth as the finest in England, and his servant measured it as 46 yards long and 22 yards wide.

Curious visitors to Wigglesworth were directed to the "sulphur spa" (a watercourse between the village and Tosside is known as Stinking Beck). A Victorian writer noted: "The perfume was almost enough to frighten the gods, and even the natives have lost their 'taste' for it; indeed, although the overflow from the basin may be seen all the year round, the natives dare no longer fill their drinking cups with this tartarean-smelling, if not actually putrid, water. Anyhow, the sulphur is not injurious to the vegetation it trickles through." Extending along the hilltop to the west of the Ribble Valley is part of the new forest of Gisburn, which was established on the gathering grounds of the Hodder. The forest, a creation of the Forestry Commission, on land leased from the water authority, consists mainly of sitka spruce; the plantations are therefore dense and dark, providing good cover for wild creatures.

When the new forest was developed on land which had previously been devoted to hill farming, an Asiatic species of deer that had been introduced to the Gisburn area early in the century found a sanctuary here. Sika deer are now relatively common in the forest. Some deer moved into older woodland at the edge of Ribblesdale. The roe deer has been seen in the valley. The ancient breed of deer occupying the hills was the red deer. Old stag horns have been unearthed near Cappelside. A farmer living near Long Preston today, having an ambition to own a herd of red deer, acquired animals from one of the South Country parks and introduced them to his land. These deer are sometimes visible from Hellifield.

Black grouse occupy "white" land edging the dale, and in spring the males go through the ancient rituals at the *lekking* grounds, two males facing up to each other and displaying, simultaneously uttering coo-ing sounds and hissing. The nightjar has nested on rough ground above the Ribble. Herons frequent the valley, mainly in the "off" season, and up to five have been seen standing in the lee of a drystone wall, sheltering from a bitter northerly wind. The mink, descendant of escapees from "fur" farms in Lancashire, is now well established in the dale, to the detriment of the waterfowl.

Long Preston ("the long town having a priest") is best seen from the western side of the valley. Anyone who drives through the village sees only the buildings, but a more distant view reveals it in its fine setting—on the hillside between the moors and the water-meadows. Long Preston sends a beck to join the Ribble. In 1881, a summer flood swept away a corn mill and virtually demolished an old cotton mill. Long Preston was partly industrialised, being noted early last century for the great quantity of calicoes that were produced. It is a village with a green, though for many years the main green was covered with concrete. It has now been restored to its old state and is the setting for Maypole dancing. The nearby inn is called the *Maypole* but was once known as the *Eagle*.

The church occupies a large mound on which, in Roman times, a camp or fort was established. Over six centuries have gone by since the church was established and it is thus one of the fine old churches of Craven, sufficiently important at one time to preside over a vast parish. Within the church is a Norman font, and the woodwork is outstanding, much of it being of 17th century date. Early in the 17th century, James Knowles established almshouses and a chapel at Long Preston, and at Arnford, a little down the dale, is the earliest known example of semi-detached building in England. Arnford was a township that grew up by a busy crossing of the Ribble. The main property was built as a pair of semi-detached houses about 1690; each house had its fine and massive oak staircase. The front of the house is symmetrical, with mullion and transome windows of four lights each. Arnford is not "open to view."

Hellifield, an ancient village, stood at the edge of the marshy dale. Gallaber pond, near where the railway runs, reminds us of its former wet environment. To Gallaber, in winter, come herds of wild swans. The Hammertons were well-established at the Peel which, erected under Royal licence in the 15th century, was protected by a deep moat. There was a silly notion that an underground passage linked Hellifield Peel with Wigglesworth Hall; if such a passage existed it would have had to pass *under* the river. Hellifield's church is dedicated to St. Aidan.

Hellifield throve with the railway. In the early 1840s, this was a small village with a population of less than 300. Came the North-Western Railway, the line being opened in the summer of 1849, and Hellifield was provided with a station. The village became a notable junction in 1880, with the opening of the Lancashire and Yorkshire Railway (Lanky). Hellifield also gained in importance in the 1870s, with the coming of the Settle-Carlisle line.

The new station of 1880 seemed vast when the size of the village was considered; it was approached along a new road, and had a large refreshment room. The influx of railway workers caused a considerable increase in Hellifield's population, which in 1931 totalled 1,026. To house their employees, the Midland Railway in 1880 constructed a row of 40 houses. The Lancashire and Yorkshire Railway built a row of eight. An auction mart was opened in 1887, to the detriment of the older market at Long Preston, and the increased trade led to the construction of the *Temperance Hotel* in 1890. Hellifield thus became as shift-conscious as a mining community. You could not wander through the village, by day or night, without seeing a railwayman either going to work or returning from it. Occupants of L. & Y. Terrace slept fitfully, having to cope with a blaze of lights and shunting noises only 100 yards or so from home.

Below Cow Bridge, the Ribble vanishes from the sight of road-users, to reappear where it is crossed by a fine bridge on the approach to Halton West. The road passes close to Halton Place, the home of the Yorke family; the river runs close to the road near Swinden, and south of Nappa dear old Lanky, the Clitheroe-Hellifield railway, is in full view. A minor road encountered below Newsholme dips to the river at Paythorne, which became noted as the bridge from which, each November, salmon might be seen moving on their spawning runs. The appeal of the lordly fish brought visitors from as far as the Lancashire towns on "salmon Sunday."

The Ribble washes the edge of Gisburne Park, and the railway cuts across one corner of the Park, though Lord Ribblesdale did not particularly want to see steam trains from his house and so the lines were laid in a short tunnel. As he was a prominent shareholder, his views were respected. Soon after the railway was completed, a visitor mentioned the tunnel ends, "built in a pretty castellated style, with turrets, battlements &c. of Yorkshire stone, relieved with red sandstone dressings." The manor of Gisburn came into the hands of the Lister family in 1312, by the marriage of John Lister with Isabel, the daughter of John de Bolton, bow-bearer of Bowland. Thomas Lister, a descendant, was elevated to the peerage in 1797. Thomas Lister was a great forester. Dr. T. D. Whitaker, the historian of Craven, noted that "on a tract of several miles along the banks of the Ribble, above and below Gisburn-park, have been planted (since the year 1784) 1,200,000 oaks, besides an uncounted number of other trees."

Gisburn is little more than two rows of buildings separated by the A59; it is the home of a few hundred people, and yet it has a considerable number of catering places, being a well-known stopping place between the conurbations of East Lancashire and western Yorkshire. A traffic peak is reached when the Blackpool Illuminations are on view. Of the inns, the *Ribblesdale Arms,* built by the Lister family in 1635, looks its age while maintaining a high standard of catering. The *White Bull* commemorates a small herd of wild cattle which roamed in the 100-acre Gisburne Park until rather more than a century ago. Gisburn auction, one of the first in the north to go fully attested, has grown phenomenally.

The church at Gisburn carries on a tradition of worship which began here in Norman times. Gisburne Park, and the hall, are not open to the public, but they have made an immense contribution to local history. The Listers had risen from modest but comfortable beginnings at Arnoldsbiggin, not far from the village. The large house in the Park was built in the early part of the 17th century. Cromwell stayed here for bed and breakfast when he was on his way to Preston in August 1648. In the next century, the Listers raised troops of fighting men to help repulse Napoleon, should he land and, as related, a grateful monarch awarded them a baronetcy in 1797. Thomas, the first Baron, gave the family growing pains as he became obsessed with the idea of creating a large estate; it was his ambition to be able to ride from Pendle Hill to Malham Tarn and not leave his own property. In 1851, the northern end of that estate — Malham, its tarn and moors — were sold to Walter Morrison. The Listers loved their Gisburn lands, but they did not live continuously in the area. The first Baron poured money into the purchase of land, but resided in quite modest circumstances at Dartmouth.

Thomas Lister, fourth Baron Ribblesdale, was a man of two worlds: of high Victorian society and his country estate in Ribblesdale. A life which developed joyously was saddened towards its close by bereavement, shortage of money, injury and a realisation that he was out of spirit with the times. Ribblesdale's world had been shattered by the rumble of gunfire in the 1914-18 war, a conflict that destroyed the old social structure of the land. In his young days, Gisburne Park had its herd of wild white cattle, reputedly brought

from Whalley at the time of the Dissolution, and lured—
it was said—by music. Thomas Johnson (1882) wrote: "The
cattle were white, save the tips of their noses, which were
black; rather mischievous, especially when guarding their
young, and approach the object of their resentment in a
very insidious manner." The last Lord Ribblesdale was a
great horseman, who directed his riding mainly towards the
pursuit of game—hares, foxes, stags, being attached to sport
with deer largely by the medieval associations and the
ancient lore that had gathered around them. He found such
lore attractive. Ribblesdale, always keen on politics, and a
devout Liberal, was delighted when Gladstone offered him
the post of Master of the Queen's Buckhounds; it was his
privilege to lead the Royal procession down the course at
Ascot, and he did so magnificently, donning the green coat
of his office. Towards the end of his life, he found solace
at Gisburn. He died in October 1925, and was interred in
the family vault at Gisburn church. Two sons were killed
while serving in the Army, and thus he was the last of the
family to preside at Gisburn.

Stress has been laid on Lord Ribblesdale's sporting interests because he and friends, the Ormerods of Wyresdale,
introduced the sika deer to the Bowland district. At first,
black fallow deer were brought in, but they did not long
survive. The sika were at first emparked at Gisburn, stags
being taken to the hunting field in carts, with the hope that
after the hunts they could be collected and returned to cap-
tivity. A remarkable little "deer house" in Gisburne Park
was constructed especially for the sika's welfare in bad
weather; it has, alas, been demolished. For some years,
escapee deer lived in the valley near Gisburn, but as the
population rose the deer spread. They have now colonised
a large area, from Browsholme to Bowland Knotts, and
from Whitendale near Dunsop Bridge to the Ribble Valley.
It is not unlikely that some deer will be seen by visitors
using the network of narrow roads in the district. At the
autumnal rut, the stags announce themselves by giving three
loud whistles!

On to Clitheroe

FROM GISBURN to near Bolton-by-Bowland, the Ribble flows down a spectacular gorge. This is an area of private estates, where gamekeepers, trout fishermen and farmers are seen. In places, the banks of the river rise like an immense wall, being liberally covered by indigenous trees and — inevitably, where there are game interests — groves of rhododendron. A cave is named after the otter, now a scarce mammal on the Ribble. In one area there is a strong and noxious reek from yet another sulphur well. The last flourish of cliff before the river emerges into more open country is called Pudsay's Leap. Every district has its memories of a great family that was sanctified by power and long residence; the Pudsays inhabited the Bolton-by-Bowland area for many generations, though little now remains of their ancient home, and the parkland in which it stood is private land.

Sir Ralph Pudsay gave sanctuary to Henry VI after his defeat at the Battle of Hexham. Life at Bolton Hall in those days cannot have been peaceful, for the thrice-married Sir Ralph had a total of 25 children, as you can see if you study carvings on his tomb in Bolton church. The Pudsay who gave his name to the Leap by the river is said to have mined silver near Pendle and to have minted coins, quite illegally of course. He escaped from those sent to apprehend him by riding his horse across the park right over the cliff, where he had a miraculous escape from death. The story has a number of fanciful aspects. He could have avoided the mighty leap if he had taken a slightly different course from the hall.

Bolton church is notable for its high, handsome tower in which there is masonry of the 15th century. The village, now in Lancashire, consists of attractive old houses and farmsteads. To it, on summer days, come hosts of day-trippers, one of the annual attractions being the Boxing Day meet of the local pack of harriers, attended by stylishly-clad hunt supporters on fine horses. These are, indeed, harriers (seekers of hares) rather than foxhounds. The local sika deer are not hunted.

Bolton-by-Bowland is not on the Ribble; it stands on the banks of a beck which, fed by long tributaries, drains an immense area of clayey land. Two of the feeders are the Bond and Tosside Becks. In its passage to the Ribble, the main beck has cut deeply into a soft landscape. There is about this East Bowland countryside a hint of distant days. A wood is called Ox Pasture. It is tempting to think of the oxen being released to graze and rest here at the end of a long working day in the field. The hamlet of Forest Becks might be tenanted by a people wearing Lincoln green! Several farms are named Monubent, and Monubent Head, beside the road from Bolton to Hellifield, was one of the rallying places of enthusiasts supporting the Pilgrimage of Grace. Here, in the late 1670s, came Oliver Heywood, one of 2,000 ministers whose consciences had not allowed them to subscribe to the Act of Uniformity. As a result, they were ejected from their churches and with the passing of the Five Mile Act they were driven into outlying districts. Heywood tells us in his diary that he sought and found refuge in Craven. Indeed, the farmer at Monubent provided food and shelter, and so, at a farm where the Pilgrims of 1536 found support, help was given to a man through whose ministry nonconformity developed strongly in the district.

Holden Clough, just west of Bolton-by-Bowland, was re-nowned for its fine garden. Richard Milne-Redhead, a Man-cunian who became a barrister (but did not practise) bought the Clough in 1877, and included in the sale were the remains of two lead mines and also a "prolific trout stream." Richard's interest in plants dated from the mid-1850s. He visited the Holy Land, and wrote a book about the Pales-tinian flora which was never published. At Holden Clough, he established a rock garden at the time when the idea was novel. It covered about a quarter of an acre, comprising a number of mounds five or six feet in height and mostly flat-topped, the stone being positioned round the sides. To the garden was introduced a range of alpine plants. Richard was an acquaintance of Reginald Farrer, of Ingleborough Hall, who is generally thought of as a founder of the cult of rock-gardening. Farrer, like Richard, developed a zest for foreign travel, but Richard did not collect plants as systematically or obsessively as Reginald Farrer. Richard's son, Arthur Cecil Milne-Redhead, followed him in his love of botany and constructed a "water garden" in Holden Clough. Richard died in 1900. The friendship between the family and the Farrers continued until the death of Reginald during one of his Eastern jaunts in search of new plant species. Reginald had been an occasional visitor to Holden Clough, and it is related that one day he rolled on the ground in ecstacy before a notable plant.

From the road between Bolton-by-Bowland and Sawley, the Ribble is seen as a broad river surging grandly with a backing of wooded hills. Sawley, like many other parts of the Ribble Valley, is rewarding to the botanist. When Frederic Riley wrote a guide to the valley in 1914, he quoted from a report of the botanical section of the Yorkshire Naturalists' Union upon one of their visits, when no less than 160 flowering plants were found. Most of them grew within a short distance of the Abbey. Mr. Riley toured the ruins and critically examined them, discovering that some of the remaining walls were built largely of calcareous shale. He considered this practise strange in view of the amount of good building stone in the district—stone that was far less liable to disintegration.

The Ribble is bridged at Sawley, a village at which the abbey was founded by William de Percy in 1147. It was never a happy place. The monks complained throughout bitter winters. Their lamentations rose again during the summer, when there was excessive rain, causing the corn to grow quickly but rotting it at the critical pre-harvest stage. The Scots were troublesome. Quarrels developed between Sawley and the abbey of Whalley, which lay not too far away. Finally, the last Abbot of Sawley was unlucky enough to be implicated in the Pilgrimage of Grace, and he was hanged. A monk of Sawley wrote the curious hymn sung by the Pilgrims in that northern uprising. Little remains of the abbey. One of the arches, which spanned part of the road, and through which travellers passed, was moved to the side and now forms the entrance arch to a field — surely the finest field entry in the land.

Those who built the villages of Grindleton, West Bradford and Waddington, on the northern side of the river, had the good sense to keep them well clear of possible flooding from the Ribble. One result is that the connecting road offers long views across the Ribble Valley. Prominently in view, and looking like a huge ridge tent, with one pole shorter than the other, is Pendle Hill (1,831 feet). In this district, the A59 has achieved grand proportions. Once, at Sawley, there was a little brow on which traffic soon came to a standstill in times of snow. Now a broad road sweeps past Sawley. Traffic used to pass through the main street of Clitheroe and Whalley, but now both places are bypassed. The new roads have undoubtedly robbed the district of some of its ancient charm.

A map of the Clitheroe district is peppered by references to quarries, for this is a limestone valley. Quarrying is still a major industry. Two mounds have not been used as quarries, one of them being occupied by the old castle, which is of Norman origin, and the other by the parish church. Before Roger de Poitou built the Castle, Clitheroe was an obscure hamlet, but under his patronage it began to develop into a town of great importance. In the first year that Queen Elizabeth I occupied the throne, Clitheroe became a parliamentary borough, and there is pride in the fact that only the borough of Wigan is older in the old county of Lancashire. The castle was in due course knocked about by the Roundheads; it "was to be put into such a condition that it might neither be a charge to the Commonwealth to keep it, nor a danger to have it kept against them." The upper parts of the walls were demolished. The keep was badly damaged. Enough remains to indicate its former size and importance.

From their ancient home at Downham — a village which has for long been assessed as one of the most attractive in the North — the Asshetons have played a notable part in local affairs. Richard Assheton bought the manor from Ralph Greenacres in 1558. He left the estate to his great nephew, who had the same name. A son of this second

Richard Assheton was Nicholas, who left a remakable diary, which was mainly concerned with eating, drinking and hunting; it does give an insight into the life of a country squire in Pendle country early in the 17th century. The Asshetons have been benevolent towards Downham; they are largely responsible for its unspoilt appearance. A charity founded by Ralph Assheton decrees that a sermon shall be preached in the church each January, the preacher to receive £2 and a similar amount to be distributed to the poor.

Pendle Hill, as seen from the Ribble Valley, appears to have a knife-edge summit, whereas in fact there is a top as broad and flat as a giant table. It was on Pendle that Fox, founder of the Quakers, had his famous vision, and it was to the south of Pendle that a group of misguided, mentally-deranged women terrified the district and were claimed to be witches. Brought before the Justice, they were consigned to the castle at Clitheroe. Today, we would have sent them to a mental home, but in those days they were sentenced to death and some were hanged. Roughlee Hall, to the east of Pendle, was the home of Mistress Alice Nutter who, unlike the other witches, was a gentle, well-bred woman. Why did she allow herself to be implicated? She was a devout Catholic, and may have been protecting others of her Faith from persecution.

The river Ribble flows to the north of Clitheroe, washing against the Waddow Hall estate, which is the setting for a curious legend. Close to the banks of the Ribble, and easily visible from Coe Wood on the Clitheroe side, is a spring called Peg O'Nells Well, guarded by a headless stone figure, which is said to be a representation of Peg herself. Peg O'Nell was a servant at the Hall who quarrelled with her mistress. Just as Peg was about to leave the building to draw water, her employer called after her that she hoped she would break her neck. Peg fell on a slippery path, and died. It was related in the district that her spirit tormented the house, and that every seven years she claimed the life of someone who was crossing the river.

Less than four miles away stands Browsholme Hall, for centuries the seat of the Parkers, who were hereditary bow-bearers of Bowland. In the hall are reminders of the old Forest of Bowland (the Parkers, indeed, took their surname from their task of looking after a deer park) and a stirrup gauge was employed to ensure that no dog capable of pursuing deer was allowed in the destrict. Any dog that could not pass through this modest gauge had to be destroyed. There are some memorials to the Parker family inside Waddington church, which has an embattled and gargoyled tower erected in the reign of Henry VIII; the remainder of the building is a restoration of 1901.

Whalley stands on the Calder, a major tributary of the Ribble, and among the sheltering hills is the Nab. The monastic settlers were Cistercians from Cheshire, who arrived in 1296. A reasonable proportion of the Abbey remains to delight modern visitors. Paslew, the last Abbot, suffered the same fate as did the Abbot of Sawley—he was executed for his part in the Pilgrimage of Grace. Whalley parish church is one of the finest in the North. The great East Window is adorned by the coats of arms of local families, and furnishings in this large building include much fascinating woodwork, including choir stalls which had been made for Whalley Abbey. Crosses in the yard at Whalley are thought to date back to the early days of the re-established church in the North, when missionaries like Paulinus went on their rounds, invariably preaching in the open air. The Ribble Valley's own railway—that from Blackburn to Hellifield—crosses the Calder valley on an immense viaduct, which is generally known as the Whalley Arches. There are 49 redbrick arches, and the length of the viaduct is an impressive 2,037 feet. It cost the railway company £40,000.

This part of the Ribble Valley abounds in surprises. Not far from the railway viaduct, which is like a ponderous Victorian cobweb draped across the Calder, is the parish church of Great Mitton, standing on the former Yorkshire side of the Ribble. The church, when viewed from outside, does not seem outstanding, though it is by no means plain. Within the building is the incomparable Sherbourne Chapel. The Sherbournes had a tradition of ostentatious interment. Another feature of this unique church is a carved oak screen, brought from Cockersands Abbey, by the Lune; an octagonal font, and a leper window for the members of the leper hospital near ancient Edisford bridge.

Stonyhurst was the home of the Shireburns or Sherbornes; the estate passed to the English Roman Catholic College of Jesuits at Liege, who were having to abandon their establishment because of the Revolution. The story of how the masters and boys travelled to Stonyhurst, in the summer of 1794, is worth re-telling. They journeyed by boat to Rotterdam, then boarded a craft for Hull, where a barge was hired to convey them up the Ouse to Selby. The next stage was Leeds, from where they went by canal boat to Skipton. The party now walked 18 miles to Clitheroe, and on to Stonyhurst, where the fine old mansion of the Sherbornes — at that time suffering from the neglect of 40 years — was slowly restored. Visit Stonyhurst today and you follow a drive which is straight for over half a mile; the ornamental lakes lead the eye directly to the vast buildings and its impressive towers. The church of St. Peter was built in 1832-5, the architect being inspired by the chapel of King's College, Cambridge. Stonyhurst has long been one of the most noteworthy educational establishments in the land.

The Hodder, another major tributary of the Ribble, joins the river at a point between Stonyhurst and Mitton. By using a map, you can plot a course on a network of little roads to Slaidburn (where there is another outstanding church) and to Dale Head, where there is now a large reservoir, its northern and eastern shores holding coniferous plantations, part of the Gisburn Forest, to which reference has already been made. The forest extends to near the summit of Whelpstone Crag which, you will recall, is the highpoint of the ridge to be seen from the town of Settle.

Bowland is the name given to the tract of fells and valleys near what are now the M6, A65 and the A59. The region still has a life of its own, and its unspoilt nature has largely derived from its isolation. The name "Bowland" does not relate to bows and arrows, though some signposts in the area were once adorned by a headpiece featuring a bowman, his weapon having a taut string. Bowland may be derived from Bolland, "land of cattle." It had a Royal Forest (home of red and fallow deer) but even before official deforestation its ancient glades were being cleared for farming, and cattle were ranched in medieval times at *vaccaries*. This was long before sheep farming became the prominent occupation it is today.

For the Ribble, the Clitheroe/Whalley area is by no means the end of the story. The river flows on by Roman Ribchester to Preston. Marshes around the mouth of the river form one of the great bird wintering grounds of Britain. A host of waders, which has nested in the Arctic, calls here on passage, or settles for a few months to follow the ebb tide to feed. Skeins of pink-footed geese pass over Southport morning and evening. The birds commute between inland feeding grounds and their roosts on remote marsh and sandbar. Water which fell as slanting rain on the high Pennine fells is eventually absorbed by the saltwater of the Irish Sea.